AF481073

Kitty Ghost Goes to Town

By

JM Schultz

Dedication

To Sophie and Ryan, my favorite Lambs!

One Day after a long sleep, Kitty Ghost woke up in the shed and was hoping to hear Sophie and Ryan playing on the patio in the yard. But today, for some reason, she did not hear them. She wondered where they were. So she climbed up on the chairs and looked out her window. She noticed that it was a very cloudy day, and the trees were blowing back and forth in the wind. The sun was not shining today like it normally does.

The screen door was open, so Kitty Ghost went into the house to see if she could find Sophie and Ryan. She looked into the Family room and saw Sophie and Ryan enjoying a lazy morning, eating cereal and watching TV. "Oh, Good morning, Kitty Ghost," yawned Sophie. "Come watch TV with us," said Ryan.

But where was all the commotion, she thought. Where were Mom and Dad? Just then, Mom walked in and said, "It does not look like a very good beach day today, kids, so we are going to spend the day in Town". In Town? Kitty Ghost wondered. What is there to do in Town? Kitty Ghost was always afraid of Town because of all the people, cars and the Big Trolleys that used to drive up and down the streets.

But the kids were excited. "Oh wow, can we buy something in the stores?" Ryan asked. "Yes, of course," Dad said. "Maybe you guys can get new sweatshirts for when it's cold at the beach. And maybe we will get some lunch at the Crab House." "Oh, boy!! We love the Crab House!!" Sophie said.

Kitty Ghost didn't know what sweatshirts were or what a Crab House was, but she was excited to find out. And so they were off on a new adventure

Everyone piled into the car, and Dad drove over the Long Bridge. He pulled up to the parking lot and grabbed a ticket. He pulled into the spot and said, "Here we are. Main Street." There were a lot of people walking around. Kitty Ghost thought about what Mom said. I guess everyone else thought it wasn't a beach day, either.

Sophie picked up Kitty Ghost, and they began to walk around the Town. There were so many shops and stores. There was so much food and restaurants. You could buy everything here, Kitty Ghost thought.

The kids bought new sweatshirts. Mom bought Taffy and Fudge. Dad bought Beef Jerky, even though Sophie and Ryan think it's gross. There were people walking dogs. There were bands playing music, and you could even see a wedding party coming out of the old church!! It might not be a great day for the beach, but they were still having so much fun!

Just then, Mom said, "Who's ready to eat Crabs!!" "Yeah!!" kids shouted. "Can we wear the bibs with the Lobsters on them?" the kids asked. "I don't see why not," said Mom. Kitty Ghost was confused. Crabs? How do you eat Crabs? And why would you want to? Crabs are mean and pinch you with their claws. "Don't worry, Kitty Ghost, the crabs can't pinch you," said Ryan. "They're dead!!"

They all sat down at the table, and the waitress rolled out the brown paper on the table. And then she dropped a huge bucket of steamed crabs and crab legs on the table. Not all kids like to eat crabs, but Sophie and Ryan love them!!! Kitty Ghost watched as the kids cracked open the crabs with hammers and nutcrackers

Kitty Ghost felt a little skeptical, but they smelled delicious!! What a feast!! Crabs and clams and corn, and then they all cleaned their hands with lemon water and handi wipes. Everyone was so stuffed.

They had such a fun day. Kitty Ghost thought to herself as they drove home from Town. There are a lot of ways to have fun at the beach!! Even if it's not a beach day!!!!